Ry's
Wry
Rhymes

Ryan Gibson

For Jenny, for Wren, forever

POSTERITY

Had a desire, desired did he
To add, just for posterity,
Some unique line, rhyme or verse
To the content of the universe

NO MORE DRAGONS

The blacksmith sighed as he reasoned why he now saw so few dragons
Those mighty beasts once ruled the sky with fire, wing and talon

The greed of man had played a hand, he reasoned to himself,
For bounties placed on dragon heads could fetch a man much wealth

It's true he also knew a few who hunted them for glory
In hope the bards might sing of them or scribe them into story

Some men would kill just for the thrill, he then thought with a frown,
Their senseless acts of violence driving dragon numbers down

But his own deeds, he must concede, were at the root of blame
For he had forged those lethal swords time and time again

The blacksmith sighed and now knew why he now saw so few dragons
Those mighty beasts once ruled the sky with fire, wing and talon

MAD PROFESSOR

Mad professor Rasmuss Moss
Was dealing with financial loss
Despite all of his best intentions
No one wanted his inventions

His melody maker, for example,
Made a 'lovely' music sample
But all who heard its 'tune' agreed
Its noise could cause one's ears to bleed

His waffle wanger would accurately
Fire pastry treats from A to B
But nobody could really see
Its purpose, nor necessity

His bovine lotion is banned now
It caused a controversial row
For no one knew quite why nor how
They'd need to lubricate a cow

His olive polish dental cream
Had indeed caused quite the scene
Although it left teeth nice and clean
It permanently stained them green!

Finally came a breakthrough, though,
To solve his monetary woe
The answer hit him with a flash
He'd simply invent his own cash

Now Rasmuss is a millionaire
And lives his life without a care
His green grin beams and people stare
As he wangs his waffles through the air

ROSITA SANCHEZ VS DEATH

When Rosita Sanchez turned 94
She knew that she wasn't too far from Death's door
So she resolved to do something she'd wished long before
To become a world wrestling pro luchador

She trained long and hard every day, and each night,
Perfected her skills and won every fight
To all her opponents it soon became clear
That she'd be the world champ in less than a year

A disgrace to the wrestling fraternity!
An old lady champ - we can't let this be!
And so a devious plot was hatched
That poor Rosy Sanchez was to be dispatched

Death came by the way of a poisoned fajita
That the cowardly dastards prepared for Rosita
But as her world went dark and she saw the white light
She refused to fade quietly into the night

Miss Sanchez was scheduled for one final fight!

There in the corner appeared the Grim Reaper
With a wicked grin he lurched at Rosita
But she flipped to the left, took a dive to the right
Then she kicked and she punched him with all of her might!

The reaper had never experienced such pain
Rosita attacked him again and again
But finally he caught her off guard by surprise
And then struck her down with the butt of his scythe

With a flick of his wrist he then cast a dark spell
And opened before her a gateway to hell
Rosita could see what the reaper had planned,
But thought to herself, 'Muerte be damned!'

With one final push she took a big flip
Landed behind him and gave a great kick!
Into the vortex fell the grim reaper
Leaving behind a triumphant Rosita

But what happened next was quite hard to describe
Rosita remained neither dead nor alive
Now she exists on a limbo like plane
Though she's quite content there and continues to train

I did once hear some people say
She can sometimes be seen down old Mexico way
Miss Sanchez appears, one of them said,
Just one night a year on the day of the dead

Still opponents and challengers all try to beat her,
But no one comes close to defeating Rosita,
The immortal champion that the people adore,
Rosita Sanchez, El Luchador!

THE FINAL COMMAND

Draw the bows
Prime the bolts
Load all of the catapults
Ready the mighty trebuchet
Steady your aim
Steady I say!

For here they come
Swords in hand
The rotting armies of the damned
We'll send them back to hell this day
Back with them
Back I say!

Let fly the arrows
Let loose the bolts
Unleash all of the catapults
Launch the mighty trebuchet
Fire them all
Fire I say!

THE GERBIL KING

Oh my Lord
Oh mercy me
The gerbil king is coming for me!

Eyes so black
Teeth so white
I think that I might die of fright

Oh my Lord
What can we do
The gerbil king is coming for you!

So close now
For heaven's sake
Hear the squeaky noise he makes

Oh my Lord
There is no hope
The gerbil king will take us both!

I see him now
God help us all
The gerbil king is …. really small!

… and actually, quite cute and fluffy. I think I'll pop him in my pocket and take him home with me.

8

THE PORK MAIDEN

Porcine beauty, piggy fair!
Ruddy cheeked and chinny haired

Enormous buttocks plump and round
Her pungent odour quite profound

Snouty oinker, squinty eyed
Rotund queen of countryside

Oh pork maiden, please be mine
Be my stinky concubine!

THE GREEN KING

He wears a crown of antler bone
Needs no castle, court nor throne
He calls the field and forest home
The green king waits and waits alone

Waiting as the winds are blown
Waiting as the seeds are sewn
Waiting as the crops are grown
Waiting for the song bird's tone

For sing she shall, not if, but when
A call to each and all of them
The plants, the beasts, the birds and men
Will know the king shall rise again

PIGGY DOG COW

The Piggy Dog Cow was a curious creature
Strange to say the least
In all my years of milking
I'd not known such a beast

One day I tried to milk it
But, much to my alarm,
It turned to me - said, "Oink, Moo, Woof"!
And bolted from my barn

FARMER PALMER'S LAMA

Farmer Palmer had a Lama
Which he fed on sliced banana
Looking sad the Lama said
"I'd much prefer brown bread instead"

VICTORIAN EMPORIUM

The Victorian Emporium of Doctor Charles Gregorian
Stocks periodic elements: Beryllium to Bohrium

He stores them alphabetically, for optimum proficiency,
So buy your Bismuth 83 from good old doctor Gregory

THE BELOW GIRL

The girl beneath the upside down
Frowns her smile and smiles her frown
She's back to front - her front is back,
Her black and white are white and black
Starts with dessert, eats starters last
Her past is future, future past

Unwalks her dog three times a day
Without a lead, she leads the way
Her bright is dark, her darkness bright
Her right is left and left is right
Time now to leave, so wave hello,
And greet goodbye the girl below

MECHANICAL

Mechanical boy and mechanical girl
Lived mechanical lives in mechanical world

A mechanical future
A mechanical past
Each mechanical day
The same as the last

Then mechanical girl discovered a spark
Deep within her mechanical heart

Shared it with mechanical boy
Now they live in mechanical joy

in mechanical joy
in mechanical joy
in mechanical joy...

CHICKEN BOY

The carnival rolled into town
The people flocked from miles around
Just for the chance to glimpse a view
Of the chicken boy of Timbuktu

Come and see the feathered freak
His winged arms and shiny beak
Feed him corn to make him dance
You'll be enthralled, you'll be entranced

Quite sadly though I have to say
That he was never born this way
They took him at an early age
And locked him up within a cage

They replaced his jaw with an ivory beak
And removed his tongue so he might not speak
His legs they opted to resize
By grafting feet direct to thighs

They plucked out all his natural hair
Inserted feathers here and there
The hands just simply had to go
So each arm was lopped at the elbow

Dear God, Dear God what have they done?
Just look at what he had become!
He must escape - Escape right now
Reverse this madness too, somehow!

When the people gathered round to see
He'd beg for help and sob and plea
He'd try to gesture, try to talk
Instead he'd simply flap and squawk

However things aren't all that bad
For our performing poultry lad
As years passed by he learned the joy
Of being a weird chicken boy

He's famous now around the world
And loved by many boys and girls
And if he doesn't misbehave
They let him keep the eggs he lays

THE BEAST

The beast that sleeps beneath the stairs
Has strong bright teeth and long dark hairs

Between the slats she peers out
With big round eyes and sniffy snout

Beasty fast, oh beasty quick
She chasey squirrel, ball and stick

Then snuggle time in front of telly
Cuddle beasty - scratch her belly

Stinky, lovely, loyal canine
I love this beastly beast of mine

LEVIATHAN

Gather boys and listen ye well
I have for thee a tale to tell
For I have seen things from the deep
To chill thy bones and make flesh creep

"Leviathan" they call it, son
A beast of epic scale
Far deadlier than any shark
Far bigger than a whale!

With tentacles like octopi
But with hooks that tear and rip
The damn thing took us by surprise
And almost sank my ship

'Twas a dark and stormy night
We'd been swept off course
And in our bleak confusion
It hit us with full force

The first strike took down half the mast
The second half the crew
It grabbed my men then each of them
It dragged into the blue

So I roared the order to counter attack
Above the wash and wave
'I command thee, men - condemn this beast
Unto a briney grave!'

Swords were swung, pistols shot
Cannons fired at will
At last the beast exposed its head
Ready for the kill

'Twas then I seized my final chance
And with my harpoon I did lance
The beast directly in the eye!
It let out a great mournful cry....

And sank beneath the waves again
Back to the hell from whence it came

Days it took to make repairs
And limp back into port
We survived to sail again
But I leave you with this thought

Leviathan survived as well
It waits for you and me
So you beware and you take care
When out there on that sea

GREY

The grey men came to gather together
Remarked upon unremarkable weather
They like to know the day this way
Dark and dull and cold and grey

Grey suits, grey hats, grey shirts and ties
All colours, truly, they despise
Each day they pray a grey sunrise
Will permanently grey the skies

Foreboding is their presence here
Once they're gone the skies will clear
Until that day this way they'll stay
Dark and dull and cold and grey

MARTIAN PRAYER

If clouds of red form overhead
And sands fall from the sky
Remember true the Earth so blue
And pray that you don't die

And if those sands slip through your hands
As you draw final breath
Remember true the Earth so blue
And pray for life in death

PEARL

The world can be your oyster
Or it can be your toilet
Depends on how you treat it
So please try not to spoil it!

IN THE KNOW

There are known knowns (the knowns we know)
And known unknowns, as well
As far as unknown unknowns, though,
One simply cannot tell

MISTER TWISTER

Mister Twister the sinister man
Has a sinister mind with sinister plans
He creeps around the house at night
In the shadows, out of sight

Sees them sleeping in their beds
Longs to twist their arms and legs
Pop the joints and bleed the reds
Twist the faces from their heads

Instead he waits and bides his time
Whilst his plans can be refined
And, as he plots each evil crime
It twists and twists his twisted mind

RUTH

Let me tell you of a story
Set in 1825
Of a village in West Yorkshire
Where not a soul survived

The children started vanishing
Went missing one by one
First Peter, Mark then Mary
Then Enid, James and John

The only child remaining
An orphan girl called Ruth
Knew what had transpired
She knew the grizzly truth

But no one would believe her
Of the tales that she told
That a beast, with eyes ablaze,
Ate up their children whole

So the villagers conspired
A militia they did form
They'd protect this troubled girl
To each this oath was sworn

And so at night with pitchforks
They amassed within the barn
Confident that all their plans
would keep her safe from harm

Little did they realise
Their scheme had one great flaw
Indeed, they'd sealed their own fate
Behind that old barn door

For the monster was not outside
No. It was sealed within
And, as her eyes lit up with fire
Ruthy gave a grin!

GUNTHER GREENE

Gunther Greene, Gunther Greene
The fattest man you've ever seen
Greasy, greedy and obscene
Cruel and smelly and shallow and mean

His big round head had but one job
That balding, fleshy sphere
Would fire commands to his great gob
To chomp and chew and sneer

His hulking bulk of body mass
He dragged from place to place
And all things edible, first to last
He'd stuff into his face

He got trapped within a lift one day
Well and truly stuck
He snarled and yelled and bashed away
Alas, he had no luck

And after half an hour past
Hunger began to loom
Then panic hit - he could not last
Oh what could he consume?

He looked down at his porky feet
And wondered for a while
'I bet they'd make a tasty treat'
He pondered with a smile

So he removed his sweaty socks
First the left then right
Placed each trotter in his chops
And took a massive bite

It hurt - but oh it tasted good!
Then licking his fat lips
He decided that he may as well
Eat right up to his hips

He proceeded with the grizzly feast
And would not stop just there
This ravenous self-eating beast
Continued without care

His belly was the next to go
Then the fingers off each hand
He continued then to each elbow
Consequence be damned

And when the engineers arrived
To discover the ghastly scene
The only thing left there inside
Was the head of Gunther Greene

THE DRUNKEN DOCTOR

Doctor Dews enjoyed the booze, adored a little drinky
With each sup, up from his cup, he'd lift his little pinky

He'd often begin with a bacardi and gin and drink 'til it was gone
Then it was time for a fine red wine (which wouldn't last too long)

Vodka, martini, champagne bellini - he'd quaff them all away
But if the poor fellow drank one limoncello, he'd be ill for the rest of the day!

PURPLE GOAT

I do declare it would be rare
To see a goat with purple hair

And, then again, much rarer still
If it had wings and flew at will

ELASTIC BOY

Elastic boy, fantastic boy - he'd stretch this way and that
One day, though, he stretched too far, and ended with a 'snap'!

HAIRY SNIFFER

The hairy sniffer sauntered slowly
To the foody room
And snooty sniffed the goodly whiffs
Her muncher might consume

The swirly whirly twirly
Tasty-tasty smells arose
So hairy sniffer snooty sniffed
And sniffed her snooty nose

Beefyness came wafting up
Up from the bubble pot
The hairy sniffer quite liked this sniff
And sniffed it quite a lot

The pingy thing then did a ping
To snifferson's surprise
She sniffed then with a wondering
At what it spun inside

The Momma thing then came in
And opened oven door
Releasing sniffs of chickeness
The snoot did so adore

Momma took some chicken
And cooled it for a while
Then offered some to snifferson
With a kindly smile

So hairy sniffer's muncher
Munched upon the chicken treat
Then hairy sniffer sauntered off
Feeling most replete

ODE TO A TARDIGRADE

The tardigrade is a tiny creature
far too small to see
But if you could, I'm sure you would
agree it's quite lovely

It has 8 arms, or are they legs?
And a tiny snout
And when observed by microscope
It seems to float about

Splashing and relaxing
In a subatomic sea
Oh, to be a tardigrade
How lovely it must be!

I WANT

The Molly-coddled mummy's boy was wrapped in cotton wool
And fed a diet of tasty treats each day 'til he was full

He wore the finest tailoring provided in the land
And mother dear would persevere to fulfil each demand

"I want a silver tricycle, a fluffy teddy bear
I want a giant piggy bank and fancy underwear

A jewel encrusted spinning top, a ruby croquet ball
And I want a little servant boy at my beck and call

I want to own a golden pig and a golden cow
I want, I want, I want it all - and I want it now!"

And whatever that he wanted for his mother would make so
But so it was with each new gift his greed would only grow

The exhausted mother tried so hard
To please her child in vain
But driven mad and sad through stress
She slowly went insane

The nice men in white coats came then
They whisked her far away
And he was made a ward of state
later that same day

They repossessed all of his things
For she'd accrued great debts
And so he learned the hardest way

POOCHY

Poochy, poochy - you're a poochy poo
You're so furry, I'm in love with you
(But you also tend to smell like poo, too!)

THE END

This truth I share with you, my friends,
That for life's starts there must be ends
Know at this end, though we depart,
Each end may yet lead to a start

THE SMILER

The trodden track that's walked no more
Leads to the shack with broken door
And if you were to peer inside
You'd fear the Smiler smiling wide

Smiling wide his ghastly grin
From cheek to cheek, and nose to chin
Too many teeth within his head
Each one extracted from the dead

"Come and see, come and see!
Oh, won't you share a smile with me?
Spare a tooth - you have plenty.
Give me a grin. I'll set you free!"

You try to run, but oh, his eyes,
They swirl and twirl and hypnotise
And as your mouth falls open wide
He licks his lips and peers inside

And, as his cold hands clasp your throat
He's smiling while you gasp and choke
Then, just before your world turns black
You realise you're smiling back

HUMAN DING-A-LING

He was half man, he was half thing
He was a human ding-a-ling!

He'd prance and dance and laugh and sing
He was a human ding-a-ling!

With a dinging here and a ringing there
And a ding-a-ling-a-ling without a care

He was half man, he was half thing
He was a human ding-a-ling!

DAMNATION

For some time now he had known
Felt the thing as it had grown
Pulsing deep within his chest
Without ceasing, without rest

Felt it coursing through each vein
Chilling spine and rotting brain
It left a bitter taste within
His mouth, and smell upon his skin

And when he slept it would awake
And when he woke his head would ache
To separate the misery
Of nightmare from reality

He felt it looking through his eyes
Heard it whispering its lies
And he knew soon that there would be
More of it and less of he

So he journeyed to a sacred place
To seek redemption, pray for grace
But as he stepped on hallowed ground
His head filled with a screeching sound

His limbs began to twist and writhe
Contorted by the thing inside
But as his bones began to crack
With great conviction he fought back

He knew not what foul manner of sin
Had drawn this vile corruption in
But he vowed aloud in his God's name
This day this demon would be slain

With that he took his sword his hand
Roared "Better dead than to be damned!"
And with his last ounce of control
Struck at his heart to save his soul

THE GIRL WHO KNEW TOO MUCH

Millie Monroe would grow to know each and every fact
She could retain them in her brain where they'd remain intact

Chemistry, philosophy, physics, maths and art
Equations, trig and algebra - she knew it all by heart

She had a love for languages, and fluently she'd speak;
Urdu, German, Mandarin, Japanese and Greek

Astronomy, biology, trivia and sport
She studied every discipline, learnt all that could be taught

History, geography, medicine and law
She'd read up on every book and then make room for more

But a strange thing started happening to little Millie's head
It began to grow an inch, or so, with each new book she read

With each page turned and new fact learned, a marked increase in size
The volume of her massive skull ballooned before one's eyes

The surgeons, priests and doctors could simply not agree
Upon a way to save the day and help our poor Millie

'Amputation!', 'Exorcism!', 'Lance it like a pimple!'
But Millie found those comments to be stupid, silly and simple

She knew of a medical library that would contain a wealth
Of facts on brain anatomy she could research herself

The problem, of course, here was as she began to read
That already swollen head of hers increased in size at speed

But Millie knew with certainty the answer must be here
So she took a look through every book without a hint of fear

She'd found it! The solution!
Then as her head grew - just a touch
There came a worrying, audible 'pop'
...she simply knew too much

ANGRY SOW

He pines and moans and groans and whines
This fat procrastinating swine
A schadenfreudian specimen
With balding head and double chin

He likes to keep his glasses clean
And shine and gleam oh so pristine
So all he sees he might despise
With those contemptuous piggy eyes

A master of hypocrisy
A dedicate to lethargy
This bitter pig - behold him now
He is no man, but angry sow

YOU CAN'T CATCH A SQUIRREL WITH A STICK IN YOUR MOUTH

Oh, you can't catch a squirrel with a stick in your mouth
No you can't catch a squirrel with a stick in your mouth
You can chase them north, east, west and south
But you can't catch a squirrel with a stick in your mouth

BORING BRIAN

He was a boring man
Boring Brian was his name
He lived a dull and boring life
Each boring day the same

He'd get up at board o'clock
Roll from his boring bed
Stroll to his boring mirror
And inspect his boring head

He'd scrutinise his boring face
His nose, his lips and eyes
He'd sigh at his reflection
And feel proper bored inside

Too bored to go to work
Too bored to want to play
Too bored to get back into bed
So he'd stay there bored all day

Bored of his existence
Eventually he died
Cause of death; bored to death
Just bored to death inside

TO BE A TREE

Oh how I'd love to be a tree
On a sunny summer day
And feel the breeze blow through my leaves
As my branches gently sway

I'd befriend the creatures of the wood
And they would befriend me
They could live within my foliage
And never be lonely

But I'd also want two big red eyes
And a massive spikey jaw
And be able to uproot myself
And stomp along the floor

The creatures of the forest
Would bow down to my command
And serve as faithful warriors
In my army of the damned

We'd enslave the human forces
Then maybe just for fun
We'd poke at them with some sharp sticks
As we danced in the sun

Oh how I'd love to be a tree
On a sunny summer day
And feel the breeze blow through my leaves
As my branches gently sway

THE KNOT MAN

Not a man the Knot Man
Not a man his he
They bound his wrists up tightly
Then they hung him from a tree

Hung him there upon the tree
Hung him there for to all to see
Let him hang eternally
This man with no humanity

Not a man the Knot Man
This monstrosity
He made no sound as he was bound
And hung upon the tree

They hung him there to be forgot
Hung him there, let him rot
Not a man the Knot Man
Not a man... Not

LADY LABRADOR

Dog lady, dog lady - the lady with the dogs
Her superpower's to talk for hours in lengthy monologues
'Bore inspiring' anecdotes of her four legged pets
Everything from house training to visits to the vets

"Scranton chased his tail! Ruprect did a wee! Luna's brand new raw beef
diet makes her coat fluffy!
Sparkle sniffed her bottom, then Bronson sniffed it too!
Barney barked for hours after eating his own poo!"

She parades them all in convoy up and down the street
All nine faithful canines trotting slowly at her feet
If you're lucky enough to meet her you must greet her and adore
Her wondrous fur babies - All hail Lady Labrador!

BEING HUMAN

Being human isn't easy
And it isn't always fun
Whether you're a father,
Mother, daughter or a son

But we're the planet's dominant species
So don't feel sad, be glad...
You're not a donkey or a chicken
Being human ain't so bad

A MAN

I ask you son
What have you done
That you might be called a man?

I strived to do good
I did what I could
May my actions define who I am

ZEBRA?

Be that a zebra?
Yay, of course
Nay, 'tis but a painted horse!

A GOOD DEED

Each morning ask yourself and say
'What good can I do this day?'
And if by nightfall you succeed
Be proud of what you have achieved

HEALTH AND WELLBEING

What doesn't kill you makes you stronger
Doesn't always quite apply
You might be healthier for longer
By just trying not to die

NOW?

If then was now and now was then
Then when would then be now again?

NONSENSE!

Nonsense is important
Nonsense is for free
Therefore a lack of nonsense is nonsensical to me
(Strawberries)

JUST IMAGINE

Imagine if we could imagine that we could imagine things together
I imagine that what we'd imagine would be the best imagining ever

PRINSTON PORT

Spare a thought for Prinston Port
The man composed of ham
He slipped into a sandwich
And was eaten with Edam

THE GROTESQUE SLIME PARADE

It happens once a year
On the dankest, darkest night
Should you care to venture there
Beware, keep out of sight

And know that what you'll see
Would leave the bravest hearts dismayed
Prepare to bear a witness to
The grotesque slime parade

Follow the dead river bed
Meet the stagnant creek
Pass the rotten cotton mill
To the swamp of which I speak

Seek refuge before nightfall
As the light begins to fade
For soon the moon will loom above
The grotesque slime parade

So it begins the mist draws in
Within your field of view
You glimpse the odd small gastropod
A slug, a snail or two...

Then suddenly their numbers surge
You fight the urge to run
For it's too late you can't escape
The slime parade's begun

Writhing, sliding from the swamp
You can't believe your eyes
This seething mass of tentacles
Keeps doubling in size

Great waves of revulsion
As they pulsate and cascade
But you're drawn to the compulsion
Of the grotesque slime parade

Then in amongst the putrescence
Your eye spies something more
Something almost humanesque
Seething in the gore

And then it stands with outstretched hands
And a gaze you can't evade
You've been seen by the queen
Of the slime parade

She's terrifying yet beautiful
You're drawn to her embrace
It's at this point that you realise
You'll never leave this place

And once your corpse has rotted
And the flesh is all decayed
You too may claim your rightful place
Within the slime parade

THE BINARY REFINERY

At the binary refinery they used to process code
Until an unexpected runtime error caused it to explode

The RAM-parts went 'Ka-Blam', destroying all the ROM
The server room went 'boom boom boom' just like a cluster bomb

The compilation station had then taken heavy hits
The discs became fragmented and the bytes were blown to bits

The unspeakable reek of memory leek wafted through the air
And blocks of ones and zeros were left scattered everywhere

The inputs gave no output
The outputs all gave in
An errant loop then recycled
The recycle bin

The solid state drives liquified
And died while streaming live
The backup tapes took minor scrapes
But looked quite cooked inside

The hardware had gone soft
All data was corrupt
The pixels burned 'til they turned black
The system had been whupped

But all had not been lost
For those clever admin men
Knew how to fix the problem…
They turned it off… and on again

HALF A JOB ROB

Half a job Rob was a bit of a slob
But an otherwise OK guy
But when work was begun he'd leave things half done
And nobody understood why

His lacklustre style could offend and then rile
A colleague, coworker or friend
And would inflict strife on his suffering wife
It drove her right to her wits end

She'd scream and she'd moan when he got home
"You don't finish owt that you've started!"
He'd shrug and he'd nod- for he knew, as a slob, it was true that he'd do
things half-hearted

Be it brewing the tea to doing laundry
Or renewing the tax on his car
From walking his dog to flushing the bog
Poor Rob wouldn't get very far

His slack attitude would in the end prove
To be the thing by which he was undone
One day, unaware, without taking due care
He choked on a cinnamon bun

All he need do would be bothered to chew
But this small task proved too complex
Hoist the flags to half-mast - may his legacy last
And pay half a job Rob your respects

63

1986

I was raised on Lego bricks
And Transformers and Scalextrics
Had Atari for my gaming kicks
And Whambars for the sugar fix

I loved 1986

Ready Brek, Sugar Puffs, Weetabix
BMX, yoyos, pogo sticks
Rubiks cubes and skateboard tricks
Etch-a-sketch and Airfix kits

I loved 1986

Roundabouts, slides and sand pits
Cassette tapes for your mega mix
Sandwich and pork pie picnics
I was raised on Lego bricks

I loved 1986
I loved 1986

SAD CAT

The sad cat's song echoed along into the cool night air
Her mournful cry, a lullaby the village were to share
For her cat dish contained no fish on this cruel, cruel day
The naughty dog, that hairy hog, had scoffed the lot away
From upon the tiles her song carries miles, she'll sing all night it seems
While old Fido sleeps soundly below and dreams of her sardines

'TIL DEATH DO US PARTS

The man with no hands
The son with no head
The mum with one arm
One kidney and leg

Each of them grafted
Onto a torso
They found in the ground
In the hope it would grow

And they were so pleased
When it came to life
They offered their daughter
Up as a wife

And in return
As a dowry
They asked for new limbs,
A head and kidney

BROKEN DOG

This dog appears to be defective
I found it in the park
It does not sniff, it can't do tricks
It does not even bark

It simply will not sit up straight
It just appears to flop
Oh no wait - it's not a dog
It's just an oily mop

MORE OR LESS

Less is more, more or less
Though more than often, I confess
To find more moreish, and therefore
Must Ask the question - is less more?

SPECULATION

I'm sceptical that spectacles
Increase perceived IQ
But with respect to monocles
Suspect this to be true

In speculating further
I elect to specify
The most spectacular of monocles
Then I'll wear one on each eye

JIGSAW BOY

Jigsaw boy was incomplete
Jigsaw boy was glum
He was missing several pieces
So he remained undone

He only had one hand
Was missing half his head
Had a hole where his left knee should be
So he hopped on one leg

He searched the jigsaw factory floor
For weeks and weeks in vain
And prayed some day he'd find a way
To become whole again

And then one night by chance
He found some bits that fit
But he couldn't see the pictures
For the room was so ill lit

Still he seized the opportunity
To achieve his goal
And super glued his new found parts
In each respective hole

But in the morning when he woke
He looked down to see
A chicken staring up at him
Where his left knee should be

Then came a grunting noise
And he couldn't understand
Why a big pig's head was there instead
Of a brand new hand

He ran then to the mirror
Chicken clucking all the way
"Oh no my face! What a disgrace!"
He cried out in dismay

Meanwhile in Massachusetts
Little Bobby Brown
Stared at his newly finished jigsaw
With a most confounded frown

In amongst his farmyard scene
There appeared to be
Parts of a little person
Scattered randomly

The pig's head was a Human hand
A knee cap took a chicken's place
And there upon the asses arse
Was the missing half
Of poor jigsaw boy's face

SIMULTANEOUS COMBUSTION BOY

Simultaneous combustion boy
Was ever so much fun
Until the day he burned away
And injured everyone

NON EVENT

A non-event occurred today
That's the word, or so they say
Yet no one saw and no one heard
The non-event as it occurred
My friend attended but I missed
The thing they say may not exist
They did suggest though that it might
Now not occur tomorrow night
If so I'll go lest I resent
To miss out on a non-event

ODD SOCKS

I would dearly love to know
Where all my blooming odd socks go
I swear to god, that something's wrong
There's odd sock oddness going on

HALF PAST POOCHY DOG O'CLOCK

It's half past poochy dog o'clock
It's walkies time it's when
We wander out, then with that snout,
She leads us home again

PARASITIC FUNGAL SLUG

The parasitic fungal slug
That lived in Hugo's head
Had consumed nine tenths of his mind
And left him quite brain dead

So Hugo owned no conscious thoughts
Nor exercised free will
But just enough brain stem remained
That he could function still

The slug was named Juan Carlos
He had survived for years
Lodged within in the grey stuff
between poor Hugo's ears

But rather than destroy his host
And find another home
Juan Carlos stuck with Hugo
For a deep fondness had grown

The fungal slug discovered
Something quite profound
That he could control Hugo
And puppet him around

For prior to Juan's arrival
Hugo had not exactly been
The finest specimen of man
The world had ever seen

He possessed no confidence
Intelligence nor charm
And his lack of hygiene
Would often cause alarm

He was bereft of social skills
He lacked both poise and grace
No ambition, dreams or values
He was kind of a disgrace

All that changed when Juan
Took charge of the controls
He'd whipped young Hugo into shape
Achieving all life's goals

Now Hugo has it all
Power, women, wealth
And in return he'd only lost
A complete sense of self!

PLEASE VACATE THE PLANET

The world is due to end next Tuesday
Fifteen minutes after nine
So please vacate the planet
And be sure to leave on time

We're all quite sad that Mother Earth
Is soon to be long gone
But don't dismay we're glad to say
There's hope for everyone!

You can choose to live on Venus,
Mercury or Mars
Or, should you select, you may elect
To float amongst the stars

REGINALD VON MONTAGUE

May I introduce you to
Reginald von Montague
The man with the plan to see things through
Reginald von Montague
What can't be done he cannot do
Reginald von Montague
A gentleman and scholar true
Reginald von Montague
He's both the captain and the crew
Reginald von Montague
His foot will always fit the shoe
Reginald von Montague
He's for the many, not the few
Reginald von Montague
So who's the man? I ask you who?
Reginald von Montague
Yes!
Reginald von Montague
Reginald von Montague

THE CHASE

We must be fast we must make haste
We're being pursued we're being chased
The thing that has more legs than us
Is gaining ground and catching up
Burning pounding in your chest
But you can't stop and you can't rest
The thing has tracked us, tracked our scent
It won't stop now it won't relent
Gaining, gaining, gaining ground
You hear its panting panting sound
Then it pounces with all fours
And pins you with its mighty paws
And you know it's a lost cause
As you face those sloppy jaws
And oh that awful doggy breath
As Fido licks you half to death

WHAT WAS WAS

What was was, was there because,
Of what was there before
Even if, if what was there
Was not there anymore

But just what was the was that was
That led to what is now?
And should we care for what was there
Or was not, anyhow?

MEAT VAN MEAT MAN

Meat van meat man
Driving to the carnival
Meat van meat man
He's a real carnivore

Meaty treats
for all to share
Gonna sell em at the carnival
And at the fun fair

Meat van meat man
Sold out at the carnival
Meat van meat man
He's a real animal

Gonna grab a victim
From each ride
Chuck them in his van
Then cook them up inside

Meat van meat man
Fresh meat at the carnival
Meat van meat man
He's a real cannibal

DINNA CHEEK THA' DINNER LADY

Dinna cheek tha' dinner lady
Dinna cheek her, lad
If ya' cheek tha' dinner lady
Things will turn out bad

Don't matter if you're rich or poor
If you're a saint or sinner
Dinna cheek tha' dinner lady
Or you'll be lady dinner!

OH MY ROBOT LOVES TO DANCE

Oh my robot loves to dance
In his robot underpants
See him shake and see him jive
His robo butt from side to side
The androids with inferior
Models of posterior
All watch on with jealousy
As he does his robo butt shimmy

Shake it shake it to the left
Shake it shake it to the right
Jump up and down and do the dance
Through the day and through the night

But oh my robot doesn't care
With his butt up there in the air
'Cos my robot just loves to dance
In his robot underpants
Yeah my robot just loves to dance in his robot underpants

TELEPHONE ZOMBIES

Zombies have taken over
In our cities, streets and homes
And on the corner of each pavement
Staring vacant at their phones

The horde arrives en masse online
With brain dead moans and groans
It's survival horror redefined
With tacky loud ringtones

Charge stations, networks, data plans,
Cell towers, WiFi zones
Those cold dead eyes, those wasted lives
Those zombies on their phones

ARROWS REIGNED

For hours and hours
And ours each hour
In March they marched
From tower to tower

Arrows reigned
In April's showers
The graves engraved
And reined with flowers

In May we pray they
Keep the keep
May good knights rest
And rest in peace

COME WHAT MAY

On his day, on this dawn
Come what may upon this morn
Be there sun, storm or shower
Come what may upon this hour
Be fate grim or great this day,
This I say; come what may

LEVITATION KEVIN

Levitation Kevin the levitating boy
Performed his levitation tricks with such enormous joy
One day he tried to levitate up high beyond the stars
His corpse was last seen 'levitating' on its way to Mars

I SPIED A SPIDER

I spied a spider inside my dry cider
I almost imbibed her today
Instead I decided to try and revive her
She thanked me and scurried away

THE GRUMBLE MUNCH

The Grumble Munch munched and grumbled, grumbled, munched and grumped
And when he'd finished grumbling he had another munch
Mumbling then he decided
"Grumblesome am I!"
Then "Muchly much I likes a munch!" He grumbled with a sigh
"Maybe what I munches on ...it disagree with me!"
"Makes me mad, temper bad, head hot and grumpy!"
Then a rumble in his tum tum made him grumble as before
So he munched another grumble spud and grumbled all the more

RASMUS MCMANUS

Rasmus McManus
A top pro programmer
Destroyed his computer
With a saw and claw hammer
His bugs bugged him so much they drove him insane
Poor Rasmus McManus never wrote code again

QUESTION EVERYTHING (...WHY?)

Once the who, the why, the wherefore
The what, the will and when
Have all been questioned pause and then
Question them again

DIRTY PERCY

Percival Pinkerton-Jones the third
Was often observed performing absurd
Dances and prances with no clothes on
Shaking his buttocks at every one

Dirty Percy, dirty Percy we can take no more
Dirty Percy, dirty Percy wanted by the law
Dirty Percy, dirty Percy where did we go wrong?
Dirty Percy, dirty Percy put your trousers on!

In court he thought they'd show mercy
If he agreed to plead guilty
To his public indecency
But they threw away the key

Dirty Percy, dirty Percy up to your old tricks
Dirty Percy, dirty Percy now in quite a fix
Dirty Percy, dirty Percy where did we go wrong?
Dirty Percy, dirty Percy put your trousers on!

STATIONARY STAN

Stationary Stan the stationary man
Got trapped in a printer in Kazakhstan
Whilst trying to clear a paper jam
He got stuck fast - stationary, man

SEÑORITA WREÑORITA

Señorita Wreñorita
con el cara muy bonita
Me gustaría conocerte
por un pizza margarita
Traime a tu abuelita
Y también una fajita
Señorita Wreñorita

SEED

Forin; a looping worker bee
Elseif; a stately ant
Pass unto them a unique seed
That they'll return the plant

LE STINKUS

I thinkus that my stinkus
Although furry, small and brown
Is the cutest little stinkus
To be found for miles around

And though I know my stinkus
May grow old and grey some day
I'll still stroke and gently poke
My Stinkus anyway

SPAGHETTI MAN

He was a blackbelt in linguine
Calzone 7th dan
He knew noodle jiu jitsu too
You don't mess with spaghetti man

I recall him brawl through a thick brick wall
Like it was lasagne sheet
The guy was over seven feet tall
And very quick on those feet

They say he gave his life that day
While fighting meatball man
Right in the middle of their epic fist fight
Came a random ketchup van

Fresh tomatoes, pasta and meat
Clogged up that street for days
And though they died, they were immortalised
In the 'Battle of Bolognaise'

CARLOS THE CHICKEN FARMER

Carlos the chicken farmer
Bought 3 chickens at a gala
He named one "Chicken", named one "Tika"
The last he named "Masala"

But their hen-pecking behaviour
Did not curry favour
So into the pot went the lot
… What a spicy tasty flavour!

SLIME BOY

Slime Boy, being made of slime,
Resembled jelly half the time
He could not really move or speak
Just sort of wobble, squelch and squeak
He met his sad demise when he
Was thrown his own surprise party
For as the partying went down
The noise drowned out his squelching sound
And given he was quite inert
His guests mistook him for dessert

FRANK

"I'd like to be a tree", said Frank
But it was not to be
He would always remain the same;
A small green shrubbery

PLEASE APPEASE PEEVED PIERS WITH PEAS

Piers appears to be displeased
Appease Pier's peeve we plea
Once displeased Piers receives his peas
Peeved Piers will be happy

WAZZOCK

The wazzock was a wazzock
Silly wazzock all because
He was a silly wazzock
Silly wazzock that he was

STEAK

"Gruel is better than nothing, agreed?"
He waited, with a grin, 'til he saw me concede
"But nothing is better than a fine juicy stake"
He continued that grin, which I knew to be fake
"So gruel must be better than steak, you confess?"
I stared at that gruel and softly said, "Yes."

LIMERICKS

There once was a man who wrote rhymes
Which were rather good often at times
So with limericks he should
Have also been good
But he wasn't

THE INHALATION OF A SMALL VILLAGE

In the village off Dull-dinkle
Nothing ever happened
Until they saw the meteor
At which point they were flattened

PASTOR PETER

Pastor Peter sadly passed
Had his last rites read at last
Over Passover he passed away
On an overpass over a motorway
As he drove over the edge that day
He was overheard to say
Over and over in some dismay
"Game over, game over
I drove the wrong way!"

DAISY CHAIN OF FEAR

The cat was scared of the elephant
The elephant scared of the mouse
The mouse afraid of the cat
As they chased around the house
Forever getting faster
Yet never drawing near
Perpetually in motion
In their daisy chain of fear

SAD MARVIN

Poor Marvin Morrow
Wills someone tomorrow
Will come take his sorrow away
Oh Marvin old chum
Don't be so glum
Tomorrow will soon be today

THE NOWHERE MAN

The nowhere man was never here
You never saw him draw in near
Didn't hear him whisper clear
Nor witness him then disappear
What did he say - I've no idea
The nowhere man was never here

CHEEBUS

The cheebus was mischievous
Mischievous such was she
She redefined mischievousness
With such mischievery

THEO THEODOPOLIS

Theo Theodopolis
Maintained a strange hypothesis
That endless bogies must exist
Up his enormous proboscis

He picked his nose ten times a day
And blew it too without delay
But to his absolute dismay
They never ever went away

PETIT PERUVIAN UNDERPANTS

Could you perhaps procure perchance
Petit Peruvian underpants
For silken dilly dalliance
In gay Paris and rural France?

THE ROAD AHEAD

The road ahead is closed ahead
The road ahead is closed
The road ahead is closed ahead
Quite why though no one knows
What lies upon the road ahead?
What lies upon the road?
It's best that you don't know, my friend,
It's best that you don't know

MOON WOLF

Said the moon wolf child to the moon wolf mum
"It's a full Earth tonight - will the wereman come?

MISS INFORMATION

The misinformation of Miss Information
The new weather girl from the news weather station
Caused an uproar with her miscalculation
Confusing downpour for light precipitation

YOUNGER

When I was younger
I'd recollect how
That I wished I knew then
What I know now
Though now that I'm older
Now and again
I wish I knew now
What I knew then

PHILIPE PHELLOP

Philipe Phellop ce magnifique
Philipe Phellop hurrah
Philipe Phellop ze finest frog
Ze finest frog by far

PERIODIC TABLE

There's a table in the jungle
Where periodically
The elephants will congregate
And discuss chemistry
They debate atomic state
With flair and eloquence
It's the periodic table
Of the elephants

VISION

The eye had a vision - a bright idea
That it desperately wanted the ear to hear
But the mouth was tight-lipped, refusing to tell
And the nose, eye supposed, knows only of smell
The skin was in and out of touch
And the brow would just frown when it knew too much
To the tongue everything was a matter of taste
But was kept in the dark, away from the face
The eye blinked and winked under such strain
And decided to leave the ideas to the brain

CHIPPY CHIP

Chippy Chip was rather chipper
'Til a chip he ate chipped his tooth
Left a big chip upon his shoulder
Chip hates chips, to tell the truth

FUN GUS

Gus was fun, Gus was cool
Gus was witty and wry
For a mushroom, he was great
Fun Gus was a fungi

THE GHOST OF MICHELLE

The ghost of Michelle
Stared deep down the well
Deep down below ground
Where her body once fell
Gone for too long
Too long to tell
Too long had she felt alone
And unwell
Time to move on
Move on Michelle...
She closes her eyes
And sighs, "Farewell"

PRINCESS PUMPKIN PANTS

Princess Pumpkin Pants
Went to the Pumpkin dance
She danced all night
By the moonlight
Until she saw her chance
To dance with the Carrot King
Romance was blossoming
As he knelt down
Upon the ground
And offered her his ring
"Oh please won't you agree
That you will marry me
And be my wife
My love for life
So happy we shall be!"
And all around the room
The flowers were in bloom
And they all danced
And kissed
And pranced
Beneath the harvest moon

BILLIARDS

"I believe it was old Pembrose
Who back in '62,
Maintained his billiards title
And defeated Montague."

"Montague was the contender, Sir,
I'm quite sure that's correct.
But surely you mean Pemberton
Not Pembrose, I suspect?"

"I recollect correctly, Sir,
Each fact I state is true."
"No, Sir you are mistaken, Sir.
I disagree with you."

"You, Sir, are incorrect, Sir."
"No. You, Sir, you are wrong!"
"You, Sir, you are in error, Sir,
And have been so all along."

"I say you are a liar, Sir,
And lacking of respect."
"And you are without honour, Sir,
And factually inept."

"You insult me gravely, Sir,
I shan't be made a fool!"
"We shall settle this like men then, Sir,
I declare a duel!"

So both men took ten paces
Each turned and fired a shot
Each bullet found its mark
Now in the ground they rot

The gentlemen within the club
All later on agreed
That the argument had escalated
Rapidly in speed

But nobody could quite recall
Just exactly who
Had played that game of billiards
Back in '62

THE SELFISH SHELLFISH

The selfish shellfish shook her head
And selfishly the shellfish said

"Every seashell I shall see
Within the sea shall be for me
I shall not share one shell I see
But keep each seashell selfishly"

True to her word, it was observed
Her share of sea shells grew
But also, too, she also knew,
Her friends grew far and few

And in the end with not one friend
All she did was wish
She'd fairly shared her seashell share
And not been so selfish

A TALKING OCTOPUS

I caught a talking octopus
Down by the port with Mort and Russ
I thought of what we ought to discuss
So I brought him home upon the bus
But he just fought and swore and cussed
And sprayed some sort of ink on us
I was distraught - oh what fuss
Oh what a naughty octopus!

RECYCLED TIME

My second hand second hand
Will still tick along
Though I find from time to time
It sometimes tells time wrong

But I still claim that my reclaimed
old timepiece is OK
For even a stopped clock
Will tell the time right twice a day

PILOTS VS PIRATES

Pilots and Pirates
May sound similar in name
But you should not confuse the two
For they are not the same

Though both might wear a fancy hat
Or hold a captain's rank
One may say "Let's fly away!"
The other "Walk the plank!"

BLACK HOLE

Innovational, sensational, inspirational machine,
His rocket was immaculate, spectacular, pristine
Flew faster than the speed of light, yet handled like a dream
When it blasted past the sky at night the sight was quite supreme

But he flew into a black hole
And was never seen again
He was lost in space and lost in time
Like a tear in the rain

We said please don't do it
There's no reasoning to it
And he knew it, but all the same
He flew into the black hole
And was never ever seen again

POOCHY

It's a wonderful day to be a poochy
Yes it's a wonderful day to be a dog
For there are lots of terrible whiffs
Of things I wish to sniff
Be there sunshine, rain or fog

DRY LAND

All alone chilled to the bone
At the bottom of the sea
Tattered sails and songs of whales
My only company

I loved those days upon the waves
My life at sea was grand
But now for all those fish I wish
I'd stayed upon dry land

THE THING IN FOWLER'S POND

Lurking in the murky deeps
Of Fowler's pond the foul thing sleeps
Each night it slithers to the shore
As surely as the night before

Squirms its way towards the farm
Through the field into the barn
Steels a sheep beneath the moon
Then drags it back into the gloom

ICE CREAM DREAM

The ice cream man's recurrent dream
The dream he dreams is of ice cream
The finest ice cream ever seen
From start to end and in-between

He knows just how it will unfold
His vision blurs, his eyes grow cold
Then staring at vanilla skies
The moon beams melt his ice cream eyes

Down his cheeks the flavours run
Into his mouth, onto his tongue
Flavours so fine that he weeps
And cries his eyes out as he sleeps

SPACE

Goodness gracious
Space is spacious
Infinite and vast
It stretches on infinitum
From first star 'til the last

CHUFFED

That chuffin' woofin' poochy
Chuffed and woofed and puffed
When I find out what she's woofin' at
Then, chuff me, I'll be chuffed

CLOCKWORK GIRL

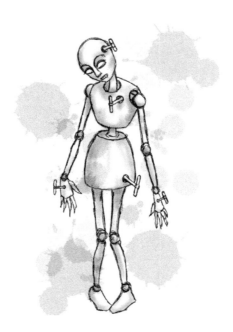

The clockwork girl had a clockwork mind within her clockwork head
She had to wind it up each day
If not she'd be brain dead

She had clockwork hands, clockwork legs
And a clockwork heart
She had to try to find the time to wind up every part

But when the winder for her hands wound down
She could self-wind no more
So she paced until her legs wound down
Then fell upon the floor

And as the winder for her heart wound down
Like some unloved old clock
The last thought of that clockwork mind was
"Tock… Tick.Tock. Tick... "

SAIGON SAM

An unscrupulous man from Vietnam
Who went by the name of Saigon Sam
Had a desire, a twisted plan
To master each sin known to man

He traded in oil, guns and gold
Couldn't sell what couldn't be sold
With what he gained his greed grew bold
His other sins then grew tenfold

He perfected gluttony
Swore wrath upon each enemy
Lusted after sloth with glee
And envied all he could envy

But Sam had failed to recall
That pride will come before a fall
His vices lead to his downfall
And in the end he lost it all

RECIPE FOR DISASTER

Deglaze your pan with poverty
Add low reserves of oil
And economic sanctions
Then bring it to the boil

Add a tablespoon of famine
A half-litre of flood
Mix in a dash of fire
Then stir it rather good

Sprinkle in a hurricane
Add earthquakes (3 or 4)
Some political corruption
And the promise of a war

Blend in an airborne pathogen
Melt the ice caps faster
Garnish then with toxic waste
A recipe for disaster

BILLY WHO?

Billy had a problem
An existential one
He'd alternate between 'being'
To sometimes being 'none'

If he was left within a room
And someone closed the door
There's a good chance he'd cease to exist
And simply be no more

Where did he go? He did not know
Just Oblivion
One moment there, and then nowhere
Nothing, nada, none

Erased from all existence
Removed from time and space
Completely gone, forgotten
Then he'd pop back into place

When he told his friends what happened
They'd think he was insane
"He's a weirdo, that Billy -
Not right in the brain"

Then came the day he didn't come back
When asked none of them knew
Whatever happened to Billy
They'd just say "Billy who?"

ROOTY TOOTY BEAUTY

She's my rooty tooty beauty disco cutie
She's my rooty tooty beauty disco girl
And she's such a little cutie
My rooty tooty beauty
She's the cutest in the world

HEXAGONS

I do not care for circle, square, triangle nor oblong
The shape I find though so refined; the humble hexagon

Oh to be a bumble bee, a hive to call my home
And live among the hexagon within the honeycomb

TINY DINOSAUR

I saw a tiny dinosaur
The dinosaur I saw
Ran across my bedroom floor
And gave a tiny roar

My roaring tiny dinosaur
Gave me a tiny fright
I hope my tiny dinosaur
Won't roar again tonight

MISPLACED THOUGHTS

Yesterday I found some thoughts
I'd misplaced long ago
I found them in a box I'd marked with
Things I used to know

The box contained more boxes
Which each contained my past
I took a look through all of them
From first until the last

Fragments of a lifetime
Stretching back through childhood
Half mystery, part history
And things once understood

Forgotten names and places
And the faces I once knew
Of things once cared or thoughts once shared
For when and where and who

We're here because of who we are
And all that we have done
It's these stories of our lifetime
That define who we become

I closed the box and placed it gently
Back upon the shelf
And hope in time it might remind
Me more about myself

LAIKA

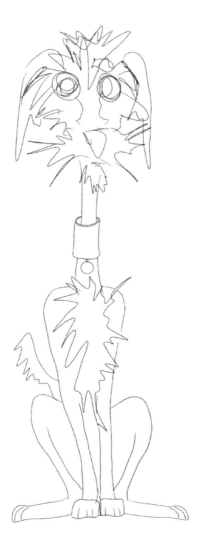

Nerry hath a finer beastie graced our God's good land
Nor dare say raced this Earthly place with effortless command

Ye may seek thee to the North, the South, the West and East
But nerry shall ye ever find thee there a finer beast

DAFT LAD

That daft lad's always day dreamin'
Wanderin' the street
Wearin' black wi' scruffy
Doggo trottin' at 'is feet

Not just street 'e's wanderin'
'Is mind is wanderin' too
I wonder where he wanders to
Sometimes I wish I knew

Talkin' to himsen' again
Wi' that vacant stare
'E looks a million mile away,
… Best just we leave 'im there.

ABOUT THE AUTHOR

Born and raised a Yorkshire lad
Game developer by trade
Ry loves his wife, little girl and dog
He loves the life they'd made

But jealous fate would enviously
Play her cruel hand one day
A cancer sent to strike him down
And steal that life away

But he vowed while he had his mind
While he still had some time
That he'd put pen to paper
And share his love of rhyme

Written within these pages
It's his last hope you'll find
A glimpse of who he once was
And the thoughts he leaves behind

Printed in Great Britain
by Amazon